The Civic Roles Nobody Teaches

How Democratic Systems Are Actually Maintained

The Civic Roles Nobody Teaches

How Democratic Systems Are Actually Maintained

The Civic Roles Nobody Teaches:
How Democratic Systems Are Actually Maintained

Richard Rawson, Psy.D., MBA

© 2026 Richard Rawson
All rights reserved.

No part of this book may be reproduced, stored, or transmitted in any form or by any means without the prior written permission of the author, except for brief quotations used in reviews or scholarly works.

This book is intended for educational and informational purposes only. It does not constitute professional, legal, or clinical advice.

ISBN: 979-8-9946881-1-3

Published by Rawson Internet Marketing.
United States of America.

Where This Book Sits On The Shelf

This book is easy to misplace. It is not a resistance manual. You will not find tactics, campaign strategies, or calls to mobilize.

It is not a guide to local government procedure. It does not explain how to run meetings, file motions, or master parliamentary rules. It is not a diagnosis of democratic decline. It does not rehearse how democracy erodes or why polarization has intensified. It is not a healing or bridging book. It does not focus on reconciliation, empathy practices, or repairing civic relationships through dialogue alone.

Those books already exist. Many of them are useful. This book does something narrower. It maps the kinds of work that keep democratic systems functioning between crises—and the roles people actually occupy while doing that work. It describes where those roles show up, how people usually drift into them, what the learning curve feels like, and why the work is harder and less visible than it appears.

Most adults were never taught this. Not in school, not at work, and not through civic life itself. What follows is not a set of instructions and not a theory of democracy. It is a description of civic labor as it is practiced, imperfectly, by ordinary people who stay involved long enough for systems to hold.

Core Premise

Democratic systems do not hold together on concern alone. They hold because some people keep doing specific kinds of work, even when it is dull, slow, or invisible.

When that work stops, systems do not usually collapse all at once. They thin. Procedures loosen. Expectations shift. Responsibilities slide from being shared to being assumed. Over time, what once felt solid becomes fragile without any single moment that marks the change.

This book is about that work. It does not ask readers to act or mobilize. It does not argue that more intensity is the solution. It does not assume that visibility equals impact.

Instead, it describes kinds of civic labor that already exist, whether they are named or not. It shows how people come into that work without preparation, how competence is built informally, and why much of what sustains democratic systems looks unimpressive from the outside.

Most of this work succeeds by preventing things from happening. That makes it difficult to recognize and easy to undervalue. It rarely produces moments of resolution. More often, it produces delay, continuity, and small corrections that do not register as victories.

The purpose of this book is not to tell readers what they should do. It is to make visible what many people are already doing, to show how that work fits together, and to explain why its limits, costs, and unevenness are not signs of failure but conditions of endurance.

A Note On How To Read This Book

You will not find a program here. There is no recommended path, no sequence of actions, and no expectation that readers will recognize themselves in every role described. Most people occupy one or two roles at a time. Many move between roles over years. Some leave for long stretches and return later. Some do only small amounts of this work, and that is enough for their circumstances.

The roles in this book are not identities. They are descriptions of recurring kinds of labor. They overlap. They shift. They are often entered by accident and exited without ceremony.

If you recognize yourself in a description, that does not mean you should stay there. If you do not recognize yourself at all, that does not mean the book is not for you. Much of this work is invisible even to the people doing it.

This book is meant to clarify, not recruit. To name, not to sort. To make the shape of civic maintenance easier to see, so that staying inside it—when you do stay—feels less confusing and less solitary.

Table of Contents

Chapter 1: Democracy As Work, Not Identity 1

Chapter 2: Why Most People Were Never Taught This . . . 7

Chapter 3: How Civic Competence Actually Develops . . . 13

Chapter 4: The Roles Overview 19

Chapter 5: The Monitor 23

Chapter 6: The Translator 29

Chapter 7: The Institutional Steward 35

Chapter 8: The Interruptor 41

Chapter 9: The Continuity Holder 47

Chapter 10: The Re-Engager 53

Chapter 11: The Boundary Setter 59

Chapter 12: No One Role Is Enough 65

Chapter 13: How People Find Their Place 71

Chapter 14: Measuring Success Without Headlines 77

Chapter 15: When To Step Back, When To Stay 83

Chapter 16: The Long View 89

Chapter 17: When The System Is The Target 95

Appendix 103

DEMOCRACY AS WORK, NOT IDENTITY

CHAPTER 1
Democracy As Work, Not Identity

Democracy As Work, Not Identity

The Civic Roles Nobody Teaches
Democracy As Work, Not Identity

People often talk about democracy as something you believe in: a value, a commitment, an identity. Those ways of speaking are not wrong, but they describe how people relate to democracy emotionally, not how democratic systems actually keep operating.

In practice, democracy behaves less like a belief and more like infrastructure. It depends on routine maintenance. When that maintenance happens, the system feels stable. When it doesn't, problems show up slowly and often without drawing much attention to themselves.

Think about roads. When they are repaired regularly, no one notices. When maintenance slips, small cracks appear. Potholes widen. Detours become normal. Travel is still possible for a long time, but it becomes less reliable. There is rarely a single moment when the road "fails." It becomes worse to use long before it becomes unusable.

Democratic systems deteriorate in similar ways. Belief does not keep procedures intact. Concern does not preserve records. Commitment does not prevent quiet changes to rules, expectations, or enforcement. Those outcomes depend on people doing ordinary things: attending meetings, checking documents, keeping notes, asking questions, explaining changes, raising objections, following up, and maintaining continuity.

Much of this work does not look political in the way people usually mean that word. It looks administrative. It looks repetitive. It happens in rooms without cameras, in meetings that draw few attendees, and in roles that rotate without much notice. Because of that, it is easy to misunderstand what actually keeps democratic systems functioning.

Public attention tends to cluster around moments of conflict or crisis: elections, court decisions, protests, legislation. Those moments matter. They are not where most democratic maintenance happens. Between them, systems are held together by routine work. Agendas are shaped. Minutes are kept or not kept. Procedures are followed, bent, or quietly altered. Questions are raised or allowed to pass. Records are updated or allowed to drift. Authority is checked or allowed to accumulate. Over time, these small choices define what becomes normal.

This book focuses on that layer, not because it is noble or dramatic, but because it is where slow change actually takes place. Many people participate in this work without ever thinking of themselves as doing something "civic." They think of themselves as parents, staff members, volunteers, teachers, committee members, retirees, or simply people who stayed when others left. They do not experience what they are doing as defending democracy. They experience it as handling something that needs to be handled.

That is part of why this work is so easy to overlook. When people imagine civic participation, they often picture visible acts such as voting, marching, speaking publicly, or organizing campaigns. Those actions have their place. They are not the whole picture. A system cannot be sustained on moments of visibility alone. It also depends on people who remain inside it when nothing dramatic is happening.

Remaining inside does not always feel like participation. It often feels like obligation. Or routine. Or inertia. It feels like continuing to show up after enthusiasm fades. It feels like paying attention when the stakes seem low. It feels like doing work that produces no clear result. Over time, this creates a gap between how people expect civic life to feel and how it actually functions.

People often expect civic life to deliver meaning in obvious ways. When it does not, they conclude that their presence does not matter and they withdraw. The work does not disappear. It is absorbed by fewer people. Authority concentrates. The system becomes thinner. None of this requires bad intentions. It happens through neglect as much as through design.

Seeing democracy as work rather than identity changes how participation is understood. It shifts attention away from how people feel and toward what they do. It makes room for limited, unglamorous, and uneven forms of involvement. It also makes room for leaving without moral failure, because work, unlike identity, can be taken up and set down.

This does not make the work easier. It makes it more honest. It helps explain why so many people feel disoriented when they first enter civic spaces. They arrive with values and opinions. They discover that what is required of them is something else: patience, repetition, attention to process, tolerance for ambiguity, and the willingness to stay present when nothing appears to be happening.

Those are not traits usually associated with political participation. They are traits associated with maintenance. That is where this book begins.

Why Most People Were Never Taught This

CHAPTER 2
Why Most People Were Never Taught This

Why Most People Were Never Taught This

The Civic Roles Nobody Teaches
Why Most People Were Never Taught This

Most people reach adulthood with only a thin understanding of how democratic systems are maintained. They may know how a bill becomes a law, what different branches of government are supposed to do, and how to register to vote. What they usually do not know is how authority is exercised between formal decisions, how procedures quietly shift, or how small administrative choices accumulate into structural change.

This is not because people failed to pay attention in school. It is because most formal civics education was never designed to teach this layer of civic life.

Civics courses tend to focus on structures and ideals. They explain constitutional principles, branches of government, and individual rights. They sometimes include historical struggles for those rights. What they rarely include is instruction in how systems are actually maintained in real time. Students are taught what institutions are for, not how they drift. They are taught how authority is supposed to be limited, not how limits erode quietly. They are taught what participation looks like at moments of decision, not what it looks like in the long stretches between.

As a result, people learn to associate civic participation with episodic events. Voting. Protesting. Campaigning. Signing petitions. Attending a high-stakes meeting. These activities are easier to teach because they are visible, time-bound, and easy to narrate. They fit neatly into lesson plans and public stories.

What is harder to teach is maintenance. Maintenance is ongoing, repetitive, and often dull. It requires attention to procedure rather than passion for outcomes. It does not lend itself to inspiring narratives. It is also difficult to teach without placing students in real settings where mistakes have real consequences. For that reason, most people encounter civic maintenance only after they are already inside it, usually as adults.

When they do, they often feel unprepared. They may understand what they care about, but not how decisions are actually made. They may recognize unfairness or drift, but not know where to raise concerns. They may feel pressure to speak in ways that match political rhetoric rather than procedural reality. Over time, this creates frustration and disengagement.

Another reason this layer is rarely taught is that much of it lives in ambiguous spaces. Maintenance work does not belong cleanly to civics, government, or political science as those subjects are traditionally taught. It overlaps with administration, organizational behavior, and informal governance. It does not fit neatly into a single discipline.

There is also an unspoken assumption that people will simply learn this work by doing it. In some professions, that assumption is partly true. Lawyers, public administrators, and policy staff may receive on-the-job exposure to procedural systems. Even then, the learning is uneven and highly local. Outside of those roles, most people are left to figure things out through trial and error.

This creates a quiet barrier to participation. People who already feel confident in institutional settings are more likely to stay. People who feel confused, out of place, or unsure how to contribute are more likely to withdraw. Over time, civic spaces become populated by a narrower group of participants, not because others do not care, but because the learning curve is steep and poorly marked.

The absence of instruction also distorts how people interpret what they see. When someone notices a procedural change they do not understand, they may assume it is insignificant or intentionally manipulative. When someone encounters a slow-moving process, they may interpret it as incompetence or bad faith rather than as the ordinary pace of administrative work. Without a basic map of how systems function, it is difficult to distinguish between drift, dysfunction, and deliberate abuse.

This lack of shared civic literacy has consequences. Systems become easier to hollow out quietly. The burden on the few people who do understand procedural terrain increases. Mistrust also grows, because opaque processes invite speculation. When people cannot see how decisions are made, they fill in the gaps with assumptions.

None of this requires a conspiracy. It emerges from the way civic education has been structured for decades. The emphasis on ideals and outcomes, rather than on maintenance and process, leaves most people without a usable framework for everyday civic work.

This book does not attempt to replace civics education. It does not teach government structure or constitutional theory. Instead, it names the kinds of work people encounter when they enter civic systems without preparation. It makes explicit what is usually learned implicitly, if it is learned at all.

That does not eliminate the learning curve. It does make it less isolating. It gives people language for experiences they already have. It also clarifies why feeling lost at first is not a personal failure, but a predictable result of being asked to do work most people were never taught to do.

How Civic Competence Actually Develops

CHAPTER 3
How Civic Competence Actually Develops

How Civic Competence Actually Develops

The Civic Roles Nobody Teaches

How Civic Competence Actually Develops

Most people do not enter civic work competent. They arrive unsure, out of place, and often by accident. They may be drawn in by a specific issue or obligation, but they quickly discover that caring about something does not translate into knowing how a system actually operates.

Competence in civic settings is rarely taught directly. It develops through exposure, repetition, and close attention to how things unfold. People learn by sitting through meetings that seem unproductive, by watching how objections are handled, by noticing which questions change outcomes and which quietly disappear. Over time, they begin to recognize patterns that are invisible to newcomers.

This kind of learning feels inefficient, and in many ways it is. It requires time spent in rooms where nothing dramatic happens. It involves observing decisions that seem to stall or circle back on themselves. It often means staying through moments that feel like wasted effort. None of this resembles training in the usual sense, which is one reason people underestimate its importance.

Early experiences are frequently discouraging. New participants misread what they see. They may mistake procedure for obstruction, or assume that a slow pace means indifference. They may treat silence as agreement, or think a decision is settled when it has only been deferred. Without context, it is hard to tell whether something is broken or simply unfinished.

Because of this, many people leave before competence has a chance to develop. They conclude that their presence does not matter, or that the system is impenetrable. In reality, they are often leaving at the moment when informal learning is just beginning to take shape. What feels like wasted time is usually the period when recurring patterns are becoming visible, even if the person cannot yet name them.

Competence also develops unevenly. Some people learn how to read agendas but not how to influence them. Others learn when to speak but not when to wait. Some become fluent in procedure but uncomfortable with conflict. Others are comfortable raising objections but struggle to sustain routine work. There is no single path to proficiency, and no single skill that transfers cleanly across settings.

This unevenness distorts how people judge ability. Fluency is often mistaken for authority. Confidence is mistaken for competence. Longevity is mistaken for insight. These shortcuts are understandable, but they are unreliable. They also make it harder for newer participants to recognize that confusion is not a personal shortcoming, but part of the learning curve.

Another feature of civic learning is that much of it remains unspoken. People rarely explain why something is done a certain way. Sometimes they assume others already know. Sometimes they lack language for what they themselves are doing. As a result, newcomers are left to infer rules from behavior. This can be especially alienating for people who already feel uncertain about whether they belong in the room.

Mistakes play a central role in this process. Most people who become effective in civic roles can point to early missteps: raising an issue at the wrong time, misunderstanding what a vote meant, misjudging how much support existed, or assuming that a decision was final when it was not. These errors are not evidence of incompetence. They are how informal knowledge is acquired.

What matters is whether the environment allows for small mistakes without high personal cost. In settings where errors are punished harshly, people either withdraw or become overly cautious. In settings where mistakes are tolerated, people are more likely to stay long enough to learn. This is not simply a matter of culture or kindness. It affects whether a system can bring new people into functional roles over time.

Competence also depends on seeing work through cycles. Many civic processes only make sense when viewed over months or years. A single meeting reveals very little. Patterns emerge when the same issues recur, when the same people appear and disappear, and when the same procedures are applied repeatedly. Staying long enough to witness those cycles is one of the least discussed but most important aspects of civic learning.

Because this learning is slow and informal, it is easy to undervalue it. People often assume that what they are doing is insignificant because it does not produce immediate results. In reality, they are acquiring the context that makes later interventions more precise and more likely to land. Without that context, even well-intentioned actions can miss their mark.

This chapter is not meant to argue that everyone should stay in every setting long enough to become competent. Capacity matters. Life circumstances matter. Burnout is real. The point is not that persistence is always the right choice. The point is that early confusion and inefficiency are not reliable indicators of whether someone belongs or whether their participation could eventually make a difference.

The rest of this book describes recurring forms of civic work that people tend to grow into as competence develops. These roles are not assigned. They emerge as people find where their attention, tolerance, and capacity align with what a particular setting requires.

Understanding how competence develops makes those roles easier to recognize. It also helps explain why so much civic work looks unimpressive from the outside. It is built on accumulation rather than moments. It is learned in fragments rather than through instruction. It depends on people staying just long enough for patterns to become visible. That is the ground from which the roles in the next section emerge.

The Roles Overview

CHAPTER 4
The Roles Overview

THE ROLES OVERVIEW

The Roles Overview

The chapters that follow describe recurring forms of civic labor. They are not ideals, and they are not a menu of actions. They are patterns of work that appear wherever procedures, authority, and shared responsibility exist over time.

These roles show up in schools, local governments, nonprofits, agencies, workplaces, and informal community settings. They appear in large institutions and in small volunteer groups. Wherever decisions repeat and responsibility is distributed unevenly, some version of these roles is usually present.

People rarely choose these roles deliberately. Most drift into them. They stay because someone has to, because leaving would mean something quietly stops working, or because they are the last person still paying attention to a particular task. Often, people do not recognize that they are occupying a role at all. They experience themselves as handling a recurring kind of problem rather than as performing a named function.

The purpose of naming these roles is not to assign people to categories. It is to make visible kinds of work that usually remain unspoken. When work is unnamed, it is easier to underestimate. It is also easier for it to be absorbed by fewer and fewer people without anyone quite noticing.

Each role is described using the same structure. The chapters that follow look at where the role tends to appear, how people usually enter it, what tends to surprise them, what the work looks like in practice, what it costs over time, and how it most commonly breaks down. This structure is not meant to standardize experience. It is meant to make it easier to compare how different kinds of work function and what they demand.

These roles are not personality types, and they are not fixed identities. One person may occupy several roles at once. The same person may move between roles as circumstances change. A role that fits in one stage of life may become unsustainable in another. None of this implies failure. It reflects how civic work is actually carried.

The Roles Overview

No single role is sufficient on its own. Monitoring without translation often goes unnoticed. Interruption without continuity fades. Re-engagement without boundaries leads to burnout. Systems persist when different kinds of strain are absorbed by different people, often without coordination or recognition.

Because much of this work is invisible, it is often mistaken for inactivity. From the outside, a system may appear calm while significant effort is being spent to keep it from drifting. From the inside, people may feel that nothing is happening even as they are preventing small problems from becoming larger ones.

The roles in this section are not exhaustive. They represent the most common patterns that appear across different kinds of civic settings. They are meant to provide a working map, not a complete taxonomy. If a reader recognizes themselves in more than one role, that is expected. If a reader does not recognize themselves clearly in any single role, that is also common.

Naming roles does not create the work. The work already exists. Naming it makes it easier to see how responsibility is being carried and where it is being concentrated. It also makes it easier to understand why some people burn out while others remain, and why some systems thin quietly rather than failing all at once.

The chapters that follow should be read as descriptions, not as recommendations. They are meant to clarify what kinds of work are being done, often by accident, and what that work tends to demand over time.

Taken together, these roles form a picture of democratic maintenance that is less dramatic than most public narratives and more demanding than most people expect. They describe how systems are held together not by moments of intensity, but by accumulation: attention sustained, procedures followed, interruptions made at the right time, continuity preserved, and limits enforced. That is the work these chapters map.

CHAPTER 5

The Monitor

The Monitor

The Monitor

Some people notice small procedural shifts that others skip over. Not scandals. Not crises. Minor changes that do not look important yet. Over time, those small changes accumulate, and the system begins to behave differently than it once did.

This kind of attention is not investigative in the dramatic sense. It is closer to sustained presence. It means noticing when agendas change shape, when language drifts, when responsibilities quietly move, and when exceptions start to feel routine. The work is not about proving wrongdoing. It is about noticing drift before anyone agrees that drift is happening.

Very little of this feels decisive. Most of the time, it produces a low-level awareness that something is slowly becoming different. There is rarely a moment when the monitor can point to a single change and say, "This is it." Instead, meaning appears through accumulation.

Monitoring shows up anywhere decisions repeat. Boards, committees, school systems, agencies, homeowners' associations, workplace governance, professional organizations, and volunteer groups all create environments where small procedural changes can pile up. In these settings, people often assume that someone is paying attention to continuity, even when no one is formally assigned that responsibility. In practice, the work usually falls to whoever keeps showing up after others cycle out.

People rarely decide to become monitors. They become monitors because they stay. A parent keeps attending school meetings after the immediate issue has passed. A staff member is asked to "keep an eye on this" because they are reliable. A volunteer remains on a committee long enough to remember how things used to be done. Over time, they become the person who notices when something feels slightly off.

At first, this feels like persistence rather than a role. People think of themselves as being careful, or thorough, or simply present. Only later does the pattern become visible. What they are really doing is holding continuity of attention in a space where attention is otherwise intermittent.

The Monitor

Most monitors are surprised by how boring the work can feel. Much of what they notice does not seem urgent enough to raise. When they do raise it, they are often met with indifference or confusion. Others may not see what the concern is because the consequences are not yet visible. When no one reacts, it is easy to doubt your own judgment and assume that what you noticed does not matter.

Another surprise is how slowly confirmation arrives. It may take months or years before a change that once felt minor becomes widely recognized as meaningful. By then, it is often harder to address. What once could have been questioned casually now feels embedded.

In everyday practice, monitoring looks ordinary. An agenda item changes wording over several meetings. A rule is interpreted more loosely each time it is applied. A responsibility that used to be shared is quietly assigned to a single person. A temporary exception becomes standard practice. None of these shifts seem significant on their own. Together, they alter how authority is exercised.

Sometimes monitoring leads to a question raised early enough to matter. Sometimes it leads to documentation that becomes useful later. Often, it leads to nothing visible at all. The value of monitoring is frequently retrospective. It becomes clear only when someone asks how a system drifted and someone else can point to when it began.

Monitoring also involves remembering what used to be normal. In groups with high turnover, institutional memory disappears quickly. The monitor often becomes the informal record of past practice, even when no written record exists. That memory is rarely requested until it is already missing.

Over time, this kind of attention carries a cost. Monitoring requires time and focus without much feedback. It can feel like watching paint dry. It can also create a low level of tension, because you are aware of changes that others are not tracking.

There is a social cost as well. People who raise early concerns are often seen as overly cautious, difficult, or resistant to change. Because the consequences are not yet visible, the concern can feel abstract to others. This can leave the monitor feeling isolated, even in groups they have been part of for a long time.

Fatigue is another common cost. Constantly noticing small problems without seeing resolution wears people down. Without reinforcement, it becomes easier to stop paying attention simply to preserve energy.

One common failure of monitoring is assuming that someone else is paying attention. When multiple people make that assumption, drift accelerates. Another failure is waiting too long to speak, either out of uncertainty or fear of being dismissed. By the time a change is widely recognized, it is often harder to reverse.

There is also a quieter failure. When concerns are repeatedly minimized, monitors may conclude that their attention does not matter and withdraw. The work does not disappear. It is simply no longer being done.

Monitoring does not prevent all problems. It does not produce dramatic outcomes. What it does is shorten the distance between a small change and collective awareness. It reduces the time between drift and recognition. In systems that last, that shortening matters.

Most people never know who performed this work. When monitoring is effective, nothing happens. That invisibility is part of why the role is easy to undervalue. It is also why systems that lose monitors often deteriorate quietly, without a clear explanation.

The monitor is not a hero and not a watchdog in the dramatic sense. The monitor is a presence over time. They hold continuity of attention in environments where attention is otherwise episodic.

Without that presence, systems rely on memory that no one holds and assumptions that no one checks. Over time, those assumptions harden into new norms.

Monitoring does not create change. It makes change visible early enough that others can decide what to do about it.

THE TRANSLATOR

CHAPTER 6

The Translator

THE TRANSLATOR

The Translator

Some people turn complex or technical decisions into language others can actually use. They connect abstract changes to concrete effects. They are not trying to create urgency. They are trying to make meaning legible.

Translation is not about simplifying in the sense of dumbing down. It is about bridging gaps between how systems speak and how people live. Policies, procedures, and administrative decisions are often written in language that is internally precise but externally opaque. The translator's work is to connect those words to everyday consequences without exaggeration or distortion.

This role appears wherever technical or procedural language separates decision-makers from the people affected by those decisions. Schools, agencies, hospitals, nonprofits, workplaces, and local governments all generate this kind of gap. Most systems are fluent in their own language and surprisingly poor at explaining themselves to people outside it.

People rarely set out to become translators. More often, they become translators because they ask a simple question: "What does this actually mean?" At first, they are asking for themselves. Over time, others begin to ask them the same question. Eventually, they are the person people look to when something needs to be explained in plain terms.

In the beginning, this feels casual. A hallway conversation. A text to a group chat. A quick email after a meeting. Over time, it becomes a pattern. The same person keeps stepping in to make sense of things that others find confusing or impenetrable.

One early surprise for translators is how easily clarity is mistaken for advocacy. When you explain what a change will do, people may assume you support it or oppose it. When you connect procedure to consequence, people may hear urgency even if you intended neutrality. Simply making effects visible can be interpreted as taking a side.

Another surprise is how often people prefer reassurance to clarity. Clear explanations can be uncomfortable. They reveal tradeoffs. They show who gains and who loses. In some settings, there is quiet pressure to soften explanations to avoid conflict. Translators feel this pressure even when they are not seeking to provoke anything.

In everyday practice, translation looks modest. It might be a short summary of what a vote actually changed. It might be explaining how a new policy affects schedules, access, or costs. It might be pointing out that a procedural adjustment changes who has to approve something or how long it will take. These explanations are rarely dramatic, but they change how people understand what is happening.

Good translation also involves restraint. It is tempting to add interpretation, prediction, or moral framing. Many effective translators resist that temptation. They focus on connection rather than persuasion. They aim to help people see the relationship between a decision and its effects, not to tell them what they should think about it.

Over time, translators develop a feel for what people actually need to know. Not every detail matters to every audience. The work becomes less about completeness and more about relevance. What will change for this group? What will stay the same? What is likely to be noticed first? These judgments improve with experience.

The cost of this role is a mix of invisibility and exposure. When translation works, it disappears. People understand and move on. When it is contested, the translator becomes visible in uncomfortable ways. They may be accused of bias, alarmism, or minimizing concerns. They can become a lightning rod simply by being the person who made consequences explicit.

There is also emotional labor in this role. Translators are often the ones who absorb frustration, confusion, or anger from others. They hear complaints about decisions they did not make. Over time, this can create fatigue, especially if the translator begins to feel responsible for smoothing over reactions rather than simply explaining.

A common failure of translation is overreach. When translators begin to add interpretation, prediction, or strategy, they risk blurring their role. What began as clarity can slide into advocacy, and trust erodes. Another failure is withdrawal. After repeated negative reactions, some translators stop explaining altogether. When that happens, opacity returns and misunderstanding increases.

Translation does not resolve disagreement. It makes disagreement possible on clearer terms. Without translation, people argue based on assumptions, rumors, or incomplete information. With translation, they argue about real tradeoffs. That does not make conflict disappear. It makes it more grounded.

Like monitoring, translation rarely produces visible credit. When it works, people simply feel better informed. They may not remember who helped them understand. They just know that something made sense.

The translator is not a spokesperson and not a mediator in the formal sense. They are a connective presence. They reduce the distance between systems and the people who have to live with what those systems decide.

Without translation, complexity becomes a shield. With translation, complexity becomes something people can at least see and respond to, even if they cannot change it.

Translation does not determine outcomes. It changes what people are arguing about. In systems that last, that shift matters.

The Institutional Steward

CHAPTER 7

The Institutional Steward

THE INSTITUTIONAL STEWARD

THE CIVIC ROLES NOBODY TEACHES

The Institutional Steward

Some people spend their time holding a line between imperfect institutions and people who no longer fully trust them. They do not pretend systems are flawless. They also do not give up on the idea that procedures matter. Their work is to keep process credible enough that it can still function.

Institutional stewardship is not about defending every outcome. It is about preserving the conditions under which outcomes can still be questioned, appealed, and corrected. This role exists most clearly in environments where trust is fragile and where cynicism is often understandable.

The institutional steward is frequently misunderstood. To some, they appear naïve, too loyal to systems that deserve criticism. To others, they appear disruptive for naming problems from inside. They operate in a narrow space where both reactions can be true at the same time.

This role appears in schools, courts, election offices, agencies, professional bodies, and large organizations. It also appears informally, in settings where someone becomes the person who explains why certain procedures exist, even when those procedures feel slow, frustrating, or inadequate.

People usually enter this role through proximity. They work inside a system. They depend on it in some way. They understand enough of its inner workings to see both its failures and its necessity. Sometimes they did not choose this role. It came with their job. Sometimes they chose to stay when others left, and the role formed around that decision.

One early surprise for institutional stewards is how quickly explanation is heard as excuse. When you explain why a process exists, people may assume you are justifying it. When you distinguish between a bad outcome and a broken process, people may hear you as minimizing harm. Over time, this makes careful language essential and often exhausting.

Another surprise is how much trust depends on tone as much as on substance.

The same explanation can land very differently depending on whether people believe the steward is speaking from loyalty to the institution or from a desire to preserve fairness. That ambiguity is part of the role. It cannot be fully resolved.

In practice, stewardship often looks like separating criticism of outcomes from rejection of process. It looks like explaining why appeals exist, why delays occur, or why documentation is required, even when those requirements feel obstructive. It also looks like acknowledging when a system fails without allowing that failure to become an argument for abandoning procedure altogether.

This work becomes especially difficult in moments of anger or loss. When people feel wronged, they often want to bypass process in favor of immediate redress. The institutional steward is the person who insists, sometimes quietly and sometimes at personal cost, that process still matters even when it feels unsatisfying. This rarely makes them popular. It does make it possible for correction to occur in ways that do not depend entirely on power or visibility.

Over time, this role carries a particular emotional cost. Stewards absorb frustration from multiple directions. They hear complaints about systems they did not design. They may be asked to defend procedures they themselves wish were better. They can feel isolated, because their position is difficult to summarize and easy to misinterpret.

There is also a risk of over-identification. When stewards begin to experience criticism of a system as criticism of themselves, defensiveness can set in. The role shifts from preserving credibility to protecting identity. When that happens, stewardship turns into gatekeeping. Trust erodes rather than being maintained.

Another failure occurs when stewards withdraw from explanation altogether. After repeated accusations or misunderstandings, it can feel safer to stop engaging. When that happens, opacity increases. People fill in gaps with suspicion. The very trust the steward was trying to preserve becomes harder to sustain.

Institutional stewardship does not mean endorsing the system as it is. It means holding space for procedure long enough that reform remains possible. It is a form of containment work, not in the sense of suppressing conflict, but in the sense of keeping disagreement inside a structure where it can still be processed.

Without people willing to do this work, institutions do not automatically become more accountable. They often become less legible. Decisions move further from view. Informal power replaces formal process. Cynicism becomes self-reinforcing.

The institutional steward does not solve these problems. They reduce how quickly they become irreversible. They keep a channel open that would otherwise close.

This role is rarely recognized as civic labor. It is often experienced as simply part of the job. Over time, though, the difference between a system that can still be argued with and one that cannot is often the presence of people who insisted on preserving process even when it was unpopular.

Stewardship is not about loyalty to institutions. It is about loyalty to the idea that procedure is one of the few tools people have when power is uneven. Without that loyalty, even flawed systems lose one of the last mechanisms that make correction possible.

The Interruptor

CHAPTER 8
The Interruptor

The Interruptor

The Interruptor

Some people slow things down when speed would make a decision irreversible. They introduce friction at moments when momentum is carrying a system forward without sufficient scrutiny. Their work is not to stop everything. It is to prevent certain things from happening too easily.

Interruption is often misunderstood as obstruction. In practice, it is closer to timing. The interruptor pays attention to when a process is moving too fast for meaningful review and chooses to intervene at that moment. This may look like a question, a request for clarification, a procedural objection, or a refusal to sign off.

This role appears in approval chains, oversight settings, committees, and any environment where decisions move through stages. It shows up wherever someone has the ability, formal or informal, to pause forward motion. Often, the interruptor is the last person in a sequence who can still change the shape of what happens next.

People usually enter this role because of position rather than temperament. They are assigned as a reviewer. They are required to sign off. They are the person who notices that something is incomplete. Sometimes they did not ask for this responsibility. It arrives with a title, a job function, or a long history in the room.

One early surprise for interruptors is how rarely interruption feels like success. Most interruptions do not produce visible change. They buy time. They force reconsideration. They create space for others to notice something they had overlooked. The outcome may still be the same, but it is reached through a different process.

Interruptors also learn quickly how personal a pause can feel to others. Even when framed as procedural, a delay may be interpreted as distrust, resistance, or disloyalty. People may assume that the interruptor is acting from hidden motives rather than from role responsibility. This makes interruption socially and emotionally costly.

In everyday practice, interruption looks small. A delayed vote. A request to see documentation. A question about whether a requirement has actually been met. A refusal to proceed until something is clarified. These actions do not feel dramatic. They feel uncomfortable. Their value is usually visible only to the people closest to the decision.

Timing becomes part of the craft. Interrupting too early can make concerns seem speculative. Interrupting too late can make them ineffective. Learning when to step in is rarely taught. It is learned through experience and, often, through missteps that carry social consequences.

Over time, interruptors develop a feel for momentum. They notice when a group is moving on habit rather than judgment. They notice when silence is being mistaken for agreement. They notice when deadlines are being used to avoid scrutiny. These patterns are often clearer to someone watching process than to someone focused primarily on outcomes.

The cost of this role is conflict. Even neutral interruptions can trigger irritation or defensiveness. Interruptors are often labeled as slow, difficult, or overly cautious. Over time, this can isolate them or make them hesitate to intervene, even when intervention is warranted.

There is also emotional wear. Being the person who regularly introduces friction requires a tolerance for discomfort and for being mildly disliked. Without support, interruptors may begin to avoid the role simply to reduce strain.

One common failure of interruption is escalation. When interruptors feel unheard, they may become more forceful or more public than the situation requires. What began as a procedural pause can turn into a power struggle. Trust erodes, and the ability to interrupt effectively in the future diminishes.

Another failure is silence. After repeated negative reactions, some interruptors stop intervening altogether. The formal role may still exist, but it is no longer exercised. At that point, forward motion becomes easier, and scrutiny decreases.

Interruption does not guarantee better outcomes. It guarantees time. It ensures that decisions are not purely the product of momentum. That time can be used well or poorly. What interruption provides is the opportunity for reconsideration before a path becomes locked in.

In systems that last, interruption is one of the ways power is kept from becoming automatic. It is a reminder that procedure is not just a formality. It is one of the few mechanisms for slowing decisions that would otherwise move too fast to be examined.

The interruptor is not a veto and not a protester in the usual sense. The interruptor is a brake. They do not determine direction. They affect speed.

Without people willing to play this role, systems become efficient in ways that are not always healthy. Decisions are made quickly. Review becomes symbolic. Correction becomes harder. Over time, speed itself becomes a form of authority.

Interruption does not stop systems from moving. It gives them a chance to notice where they are going before it is too late to change course.

The Continuity Holder

CHAPTER 9
The Continuity Holder

The Continuity Holder

The Continuity Holder

Some people keep routines going after attention fades. They maintain records, preserve processes, and carry institutional memory across turnover. Their work is not to create momentum. It is to make sure things do not disappear when no one is looking.

Continuity is easy to mistake for stagnation. From the outside, it can look like nothing is happening. In reality, something is happening every time a record is kept, a procedure is followed, or a recurring task is completed without fanfare. The continuity holder is the person who makes sure that what existed last month still exists this month.

This role appears wherever participation cycles. Committees, boards, volunteer organizations, schools, professional groups, and community efforts all experience turnover. People join with energy. They leave when priorities shift. In between, someone has to keep the lights on. That work rarely comes with recognition.

People usually enter this role by staying when others leave. They inherit responsibility rather than seeking it. A meeting needs notes. A file needs updating. A process needs someone to remember how it works. Over time, these small inheritances accumulate. The continuity holder becomes the person others rely on for memory and follow-through.

One of the first surprises in this role is how invisible success feels. When continuity is maintained, nothing breaks. Meetings still happen. Information is still available. Processes still function. Because there is no obvious crisis, the work can feel pointless, even to the person doing it.

Another surprise is how quickly memory disappears. In groups with regular turnover, what was common knowledge a year ago may be unknown today. The continuity holder often becomes the only person who remembers why something was set up a certain way or what problem a rule was meant to address. That memory is rarely written down in full. It lives in experience.

The Continuity Holder

In practice, continuity looks ordinary. Maintaining contact lists. Keeping shared files organized. Making sure recurring reports are produced. Preserving documentation that no one reads until they need it. These tasks are easy to postpone and easy to drop. When they are dropped, gaps appear slowly and then all at once.

Continuity holders also tend to become informal reference points. People ask them how things are supposed to work. They are consulted when something goes wrong and no one remembers the original decision. Over time, this can turn into an unspoken expectation that they will always be there.

The cost of this role is monotony and invisibility. Much of the work is repetitive. It does not feel creative. It does not feel impactful in the short term. Over time, it can create a sense of being taken for granted, especially when others cycle through with enthusiasm and then leave.

There is also a risk of overload. Because continuity holders are reliable, they are often given more responsibility. Tasks accumulate. The role expands quietly. What began as helping becomes carrying. Without boundaries, continuity can turn into quiet overextension.

A common failure of this role is silent exhaustion. The continuity holder keeps things going until they cannot. When they finally step back, systems often discover how much was being held together by one person. The result can feel like sudden collapse, even though the strain had been building for a long time.

Another failure occurs when continuity becomes rigidity. When memory is held too tightly, it can be used to resist necessary change. The role shifts from preserving function to preserving form. When that happens, continuity becomes a barrier rather than a support.

Continuity does not mean resisting change. It means carrying forward what allows a system to function while change is occurring. It provides a reference point for what is being altered. Without that reference, it becomes harder to tell whether something is improving, degrading, or simply different.

In systems that last, continuity is often maintained by people who never intended to become essential. They became essential because they stayed. They kept track. They made sure someone was still responsible when responsibility became diffuse.

The continuity holder is not a leader in the traditional sense. They are a stabilizer. They provide memory and follow-through in environments where both are fragile.

Without continuity holders, systems rely on enthusiasm alone. Enthusiasm comes and goes. Memory does not, unless someone carries it. When no one does, systems lose not only their past but their ability to learn from it.

Continuity does not create momentum. It makes momentum survivable. It allows efforts to outlast individual participants. It is one of the quiet conditions that allow collective work to persist beyond a single cycle of attention.

The Re-Engager

CHAPTER 10
The Re-Engager

The Re-Engager

The Re-Engager

Some people make return possible without shame. They lower the social and emotional cost of coming back after disengagement. Their work is not to persuade people to care more. It is to make participation possible again after it has become difficult.

Disengagement is common in civic life. People leave because of time pressure, conflict, exhaustion, disappointment, or changes in personal circumstance. Most departures are not dramatic. They happen quietly. A few meetings are missed. A role is stepped away from. Over time, absence becomes normal.

Re-engagement is harder than initial entry. Returning means facing whatever led to departure. It can involve embarrassment, fear of judgment, or concern that one's absence will be noticed and resented. Many people stay away not because they no longer care, but because coming back feels socially risky.

The re-engager's work is to reduce that risk. This role appears in community groups, workplaces, schools, volunteer organizations, and informal networks. It shows up wherever people cycle in and out. The re-engager is often someone who has disengaged themselves before. They understand how difficult return can feel, even when the door is technically open.

People usually enter this role without naming it. They are the person who reaches out without asking where someone has been. They say, "We'd love to see you," rather than, "We wondered why you stopped coming." They design participation in ways that do not require total commitment. They make space for partial involvement.

One of the first surprises for re-engagers is how often moral pressure shuts doors rather than opening them. Language about duty, responsibility, or letting others down can make return feel like an admission of failure. Even well-intentioned appeals can increase the emotional cost of coming back.

In everyday practice, re-engagement looks small. A personal message that does not demand explanation. A reminder that someone is still welcome. A meeting format that allows people to sit quietly before participating. A role that can be picked up without full reimmersion. These gestures do not look like leadership. They look like hospitality.

The re-engager often becomes a bridge between those who stayed and those who left. This can be uncomfortable. People who remained may feel resentment. They may question why return should be easy when staying was hard. The re-engager absorbs some of that tension by refusing to frame return as a moral issue.

The cost of this role is emotional labor. Re-engagers carry other people's ambivalence. They hold space for hesitation, guilt, and uncertainty. They often do this quietly, without recognition, and without clear outcomes. Many attempts at re-engagement do not succeed. People may still choose not to return.

There is also a risk of being misread. Re-engagers can be seen as minimizing commitment or lowering standards. They may be accused of enabling inconsistency or of failing to hold people accountable. In environments that equate intensity with seriousness, re-engagement can be mistaken for weakness.

One common failure of this role is sliding into gatekeeping. Over time, re-engagers may become informal arbiters of who is welcomed back and under what conditions. When that happens, the role shifts from lowering barriers to managing access. The work becomes about control rather than return.

Another failure occurs when re-engagers overextend themselves emotionally. Constantly absorbing others' hesitation can be draining. Without boundaries, the role can turn into carrying responsibility for other people's choices. When that happens, burnout is likely.

Re-engagement does not guarantee renewed participation. It guarantees the possibility of return. In systems that last, that possibility matters. Without it, departure becomes permanent. Groups harden around those who stayed. Over time, the pool of participants narrows.

The re-engager is not a recruiter in the usual sense. They are a signal that absence does not erase belonging. They keep the door open in environments where it would otherwise close quietly.

Without people willing to do this work, civic spaces become less forgiving. They reward only uninterrupted participation. That standard excludes many people whose lives make consistency difficult. Over time, systems become populated by those with the greatest capacity to stay, not necessarily by those with the greatest stake.

Re-engagement does not solve the reasons people leave. It makes return possible even when those reasons have not disappeared. It acknowledges that participation is not a straight line.

In systems that endure, return is as important as entry. The re-engager is one of the people who makes that possible.

The Boundary Setter

CHAPTER 11
The Boundary Setter

The Boundary Setter

The Boundary Setter

Some people protect sustainability by deciding how much is enough. They set limits on time, energy, and exposure so that participation can continue without becoming consuming. Their work is not to withdraw. It is to keep involvement from turning into something that cannot be sustained.

Boundary setting is often mistaken for disengagement. In reality, it is one of the ways people remain involved over the long term. Without limits, many forms of civic work become intolerable. With limits, participation can be carried in smaller, more durable ways.

This role appears wherever civic work creates ongoing demand. Committees that always need volunteers. Organizations that quietly rely on a few dependable people. Institutions where responsibility expands without being renegotiated. In these environments, the person who sets boundaries is often the person who has already given more than was reasonable.

Most people enter this role after overload. They have said yes too many times. They have absorbed strain without noticing how much it was costing them. They discover that their availability has become an assumption rather than a choice. Boundary setting often begins as a response to exhaustion rather than as a planned decision.

One early surprise is how personal limits are heard as moral statements. Saying no can be interpreted as lack of commitment. Reducing involvement can be read as indifference. Leaving a role can feel, to others, like abandonment. Boundary setters learn quickly that limits are rarely received neutrally, even when they are necessary.

In practice, boundary setting looks ordinary. Declining an additional task. Stepping down from a role while staying connected. Limiting availability to certain hours. Refusing escalation when intensity increases. These actions do not look like leadership. They look like self-management. Over time, they determine whether participation remains possible at all.

The Boundary Setter

Boundary setters often carry quiet guilt. They may feel they are letting others down. They may compare themselves to people who appear to give more. They may worry that reducing involvement means losing their place. These feelings are part of the role, even when the limits are reasonable.

There is also social friction. Groups that rely heavily on a few people can respond poorly when those people set boundaries. Tasks that were once absorbed quietly suddenly become visible. Others may feel pressure to step up. Resentment can surface. Boundary setters often absorb that tension simply by refusing to continue overextending.

A common failure of this role is waiting too long. People delay setting limits until they are depleted. When boundaries finally appear, they may come in the form of sudden withdrawal rather than gradual adjustment. The system experiences this as loss rather than as sustainability.

Another failure occurs when boundaries become walls. In an effort to protect themselves, some people cut off all involvement rather than reshaping it. Sometimes this is necessary. Often, it reflects having waited too long to set smaller limits earlier.

Boundary setting is also unevenly available. Power, status, and security affect whether people can safely say no. Some people can set limits with little consequence. Others risk retaliation, loss of standing, or informal punishment. As a result, boundary setting is not only a personal skill. It is shaped by context.

When boundaries are respected, systems become more resilient. Responsibility is distributed more evenly. Burnout becomes less common. Participation becomes more sustainable. When boundaries are ignored or punished, systems become dependent on overextension. They function until people collapse or leave.

The boundary setter is not a quitter. They are someone who stabilizes capacity. They make it possible for work to continue at a level that does not destroy the people doing it.

Without boundary setters, civic systems rely on sacrifice rather than sustainability. Over time, that reliance narrows participation to those willing or able to absorb disproportionate strain. The result is burnout, turnover, and loss of institutional memory.

Boundary setting does not reduce commitment. It makes commitment survivable. It allows people to stay in civic life in smaller, more realistic ways. It also signals that participation is not all or nothing.

In systems that last, someone eventually has to decide what is enough. When no one does, the cost is paid later, often in the form of sudden exits and quiet collapse.

The boundary setter's work is to prevent that collapse by setting limits early enough that staying remains possible.

No One Role Is Enough

CHAPTER 12
No One Role Is Enough

No One Role Is Enough

No One Role Is Enough

The roles described in the previous chapters do not function in isolation. Each addresses a different kind of strain. Each compensates for a different weakness in how systems operate over time. When several are present together, they create something closer to balance. When one or more disappear, pressure concentrates elsewhere.

Monitoring without translation often goes unnoticed. Small shifts are seen, but not explained in ways others can grasp. The information remains private or informal. Patterns are recognized but never become shared understanding. Drift continues, even though someone is watching it happen.

Translation without monitoring becomes reactive. Explanations arrive after consequences are already visible. By then, options are narrower. What could have been questioned early becomes something people argue about late. Clarity appears, but timing is lost.

Interruption without continuity rarely changes habits. A pause is created, a question is raised, a decision is delayed. But if no one carries memory forward, the same issue returns in a slightly different form. The system absorbs the interruption without learning from it.

Continuity without interruption can harden. Processes are preserved, records are kept, routines continue. Over time, those routines can become automatic. What was once functional becomes unquestioned. Without friction, continuity turns into inertia.

Re-engagement without boundaries leads to overload. People are welcomed back, participation is made easier, and involvement expands. Without limits, the same few people absorb increasing demand. Return becomes possible, but staying becomes unsustainable.

Boundary setting without re-engagement leads to thinning. People protect their capacity, step back, and limit involvement. Without paths for return, the pool of participants shrinks. The system becomes dependent on a smaller group, increasing strain on those who remain.

Institutional stewardship without monitoring becomes hollow. Process is defended, but drift is not tracked. Over time, the system appears legitimate while quietly changing in ways that undermine its original purpose.

Monitoring without stewardship becomes fragile. Problems are noticed, but there is no shared commitment to preserving procedure. Attention becomes cynical rather than corrective. Drift is seen, but no one holds the structure that would allow response.

These pairings are not exhaustive. They illustrate a broader point. Democratic maintenance is not carried by a single kind of person or a single kind of effort. It is carried by overlapping forms of work that compensate for one another's limits.

This is one reason systems can appear to function even when key roles are missing. For a time, other roles absorb the strain. Translators compensate for weak monitoring by explaining consequences after the fact. Continuity holders compensate for weak stewardship by keeping things running even as trust erodes. Boundary setters compensate for weak re-engagement by preventing total burnout among those who remain.

These compensations are temporary. Over time, imbalance accumulates. The system becomes more fragile, even if it appears stable from the outside.

Because of this, people often misdiagnose what is wrong. They see outcomes they dislike and assume the problem is ideological. They see disengagement and assume people no longer care. They see procedural breakdown and assume incompetence or bad faith. Sometimes those explanations are accurate. Often, they are incomplete. Many failures are structural rather than moral. They reflect missing roles rather than missing values.

Understanding how roles interact changes how strain is interpreted. It shifts attention from individual behavior to patterns of coverage. Who is noticing? Who is explaining? Who is interrupting? Who is carrying memory? Who is making return possible? Who is setting limits? When one of these questions has no answer, pressure builds somewhere else.

This shift also reduces moralization. Instead of asking why people are not trying harder, it becomes possible to ask which kinds of work are missing or overloaded. That question leads to different conversations. It leads to adjustments rather than accusations.

Systems that last are not perfectly balanced. They are uneven and adaptive. Different roles carry more weight at different times. What matters is not perfection. What matters is whether the system has access to enough kinds of work to respond when strain shifts.

No one role is enough because no one kind of strain is constant. Democratic maintenance is not a single task. It is a set of overlapping pressures that require different kinds of attention over time.

Seeing this does not make participation easier. It makes it less confusing. It also makes it easier to understand why systems fail quietly rather than all at once. When a role disappears, something else absorbs the load until it cannot.

The chapters that follow look at how people find their way into these roles and how success is measured when most of the work is invisible.

CHAPTER 13
How People Find Their Place

The Civic Roles Nobody Teaches
How People Find Their Place

People rarely enter civic work with a clear sense of where they belong. They do not usually choose a role in advance. They arrive because something intersects with their life: a school issue, a workplace responsibility, a neighborhood problem, a professional obligation, a personal loss, or a moment of concern that feels close enough to act on.

What begins as a specific reason to show up often turns into a broader pattern of involvement. Over time, people discover that they keep being asked for the same kind of thing. They are the one who notices changes. The one who explains what happened. The one who keeps records. The one who asks uncomfortable questions. The one who reaches out when others disappear. The one who says no when demand grows too large.

Most people recognize their role only in hindsight. This is partly because roles are not assigned. They emerge from a mix of temperament, availability, position, and tolerance for certain kinds of strain. Someone with limited time but steady attention may become a monitor. Someone comfortable with explanation may become a translator. Someone with formal authority may become an interruptor. Someone who stays longest may become a continuity holder. Someone who has left and returned may become a re-engager. Someone who has burned out may become a boundary setter.

None of this happens cleanly. People try things. They stop doing what exhausts them. They continue doing what feels manageable or necessary. Over time, patterns form without anyone explicitly naming them.

Life stage plays a large role. What is possible when someone has young children is different from what is possible later. What feels manageable early in a career is different from what feels manageable when professional risk is higher. Retirement, caregiving, health, and financial security all shape how much exposure and responsibility someone can carry at any given time.

Because of this, people's roles change. Someone who once interrupted may later focus on continuity. Someone who once translated may later set boundaries. Someone who once monitored closely may step back and only pay attention when something feels off. These shifts are not failures. They are adjustments to changing capacity.

People also misjudge what is needed. They may assume a setting requires more intensity when it actually requires more patience. They may assume visibility matters more than follow-through. They may take on a role because it feels morally compelling, only to discover it is not sustainable for them. Over time, many people learn to listen to these signals, even if they do not yet have language for what is happening.

Finding a place is also shaped by who else is present. When a setting already has strong continuity, new participants may drift toward translation or monitoring. When interruption is missing, someone with authority may be pulled into that role. When re-engagement is absent, someone with relational skill may begin doing that work simply because no one else is.

These dynamics mean that roles are often filled by default rather than by design. The person most willing to absorb a particular kind of strain becomes the person doing that work. Over time, this can create imbalances. One person carries too much. Another kind of work is not being done at all.

Because roles are informal, people may not realize they are overloaded until they are exhausted. They may not realize a role is missing until a problem becomes visible. They may not realize their own work matters until it stops and something breaks.

This is why naming roles can be useful. It does not assign people to categories. It makes patterns visible. It gives people language for why certain tasks feel heavier than others. It also makes it easier to see when responsibility has quietly concentrated.

Finding a place does not mean finding a perfect fit. It means finding a way to contribute that does not require becoming someone else. It also means recognizing when a role no longer fits and adjusting accordingly.

Some people worry that if they do less, something important will be lost. Sometimes that is true. Often, it is also a sign that a system has become too dependent on a few people. Adjusting one's role can expose that dependence. That exposure can be uncomfortable. It can also be necessary for long-term sustainability.

People also worry that they are not doing enough. In a culture that equates commitment with intensity, smaller forms of participation can feel inadequate. This book argues otherwise. Many systems are held together by limited, consistent contributions rather than by heroic effort. What matters is not how much any one person does. What matters is whether enough different kinds of work are being carried.

Finding a place is not a one-time decision. It is an ongoing negotiation between what a system seems to require and what a person can reasonably offer. That negotiation changes over time. It is shaped by fatigue, learning, confidence, and changing life circumstances.

In systems that last, people are not locked into roles. They move. They step back. They return. They shift focus. The system survives not because everyone does everything, but because people adjust without disappearing entirely.

Understanding this reduces pressure to find a perfect form of participation. It also reduces the tendency to judge others by how visible their involvement is. Many forms of civic work are quiet by design. They are still work.

Finding a place is less about choosing a role and more about noticing what you keep being asked to do, what you keep doing without being asked, and what kinds of strain you can carry without breaking. Over time, those patterns reveal where you fit for now.

That fit is not permanent. It is provisional. In that sense, civic work resembles the systems it sustains: maintained, adjusted, and carried forward by people whose capacity is always changing.

CHAPTER 14
Measuring Success Without Headlines

Measuring Success Without Headlines

Most civic work does not produce moments that look like victory. There are no announcements. No clear turning points. No single outcome that confirms something important has been accomplished. This makes it difficult to know whether effort is having any effect.

Many people quietly stop participating not because they stop caring, but because they stop seeing evidence that their work matters. When progress is measured only by visible outcomes, most maintenance work disappears from view. The absence of breakdown is not recognized as an achievement. Stability is mistaken for stasis.

This creates a distorted sense of what success looks like. It favors moments that are loud, public, and decisive. It undervalues work that prevents problems from becoming visible in the first place. As a result, people who do maintenance work often feel as though they are failing, even when they are holding systems together.

In this kind of work, success often appears as continuity rather than change. A procedure that still exists. A channel that remains open. A process that can still be appealed. A group that continues to meet. These are not dramatic. They are conditions. When they disappear, their absence is felt quickly. When they persist, they are taken for granted.

Another sign of success is earlier awareness. Problems are noticed before they escalate. Questions are raised before decisions harden. People understand what is happening before they are forced to react. None of this produces a headline. It produces fewer surprises.

There is also success in reduced strain. When responsibilities are distributed more evenly. When burnout becomes less common. When return becomes easier. When boundaries are respected. These shifts change how work feels, not just what work produces. They make participation more durable.

Some forms of success are defined by what does not happen. A conflict that does not escalate. A decision that is slowed long enough to be reconsidered. A policy that is revised quietly before it becomes a public problem. These outcomes leave little trace. They matter anyway.

Because of this, people often misread their own impact. They compare their quiet work to visible activism or high-profile outcomes and conclude that they are doing less. In reality, they may be doing different work. Maintenance is not the absence of action. It is a different category of action.

This misreading can lead to discouragement. People feel replaceable. They feel unnoticed. They assume that if they stopped, nothing would change. Often, the opposite is true. The change would not be immediate. It would be cumulative. Things would become harder to track, harder to appeal, harder to sustain. The loss would be gradual and then obvious.

Time also distorts perception. Many forms of civic maintenance only reveal their value over long periods. A record kept today matters years later. A precedent preserved becomes important in a future dispute. A relationship maintained becomes critical during a crisis. These time horizons do not align with how people are used to measuring impact.

This makes it difficult to stay motivated. Humans respond to feedback. When feedback is delayed or invisible, effort becomes harder to sustain. Recognizing this is part of sustaining participation. It is not a personal weakness. It is a structural feature of maintenance work.

Some people try to solve this by creating artificial metrics. Counting meetings attended. Tracking messages sent. Measuring hours volunteered. These can be useful for accountability. They do not capture what actually matters. They measure activity, not function. They do not tell you whether drift was noticed, whether process was preserved, whether return was made possible.

More meaningful signals are often indirect. People still come to you with questions. Someone asks how things used to work. A pause you created becomes standard practice. A document you maintained is referenced. A person who left shows up again. These are not public achievements. They are quiet confirmations that something is being carried.

Success in this kind of work is often relational. It appears in trust that persists. In the assumption that someone will answer. In the expectation that someone is paying attention. These expectations are rarely articulated. They become visible only when they are violated.

Measuring success without headlines requires recalibrating what counts. It means noticing conditions rather than events. It means valuing continuity, clarity, and capacity as outcomes in their own right. It means recognizing that preventing breakdown is itself an achievement.

This does not mean abandoning ambition or accepting deterioration. It means understanding that many forms of civic work are designed to keep systems functional long enough for larger changes to remain possible. Without that function, even ambitious efforts have nowhere to land.

People who do this work often need to learn to recognize its value for themselves, even when it is not publicly affirmed. That recognition is part of what allows them to continue. It is also part of what makes this work legible to others. Success without headlines is harder to see. It is also the kind of success most systems depend on.

When To Step Back, When To Stay

CHAPTER 15
When To Step Back, When To Stay

When To Step Back, When To Stay

When To Step Back, When To Stay

Staying is not always the right choice. Neither is leaving. One of the hardest parts of civic work is knowing when continued participation is sustaining something valuable and when it is simply absorbing cost without effect.

People often treat staying as a moral default. Leaving is framed as failure, weakness, or abandonment. This framing makes it difficult to evaluate participation honestly. It also increases burnout by turning exhaustion into a private shame rather than a signal that something needs to change.

Stepping back is not always disengagement. It can be a form of boundary setting. It can be a way of forcing redistribution of responsibility. It can be a signal that a system has become too dependent on a few people. In some cases, stepping back reveals problems that were being masked by overextension.

At the same time, staying can matter precisely when things feel stuck. Many systems improve slowly. Early efforts do not produce visible change. Leaving too quickly can mean that the period of adjustment is never reached. The difficulty is telling the difference between a slow process and a dead end.

One way to think about this is to look at whether your role is still functional. Are you still able to do the kind of work you entered to do? Is your contribution still making something visible, possible, or sustainable? Or has your work become purely absorptive, taking strain without changing conditions?

Another lens is who else is present. Are there others who could take on parts of what you are carrying? Are you blocking redistribution by staying in a role no one else has had a chance to learn? Sometimes staying prevents growth. Sometimes leaving creates it.

Personal cost also matters. Not all strain is the same. Some strain is part of meaningful work. Other strain erodes health, relationships, or livelihood. When cost consistently exceeds capacity, staying becomes a form of self-sacrifice that systems rarely repay.

There is also the question of replacement. Some people feel they cannot leave because no one else will step in. Sometimes that is true. More often, it reflects how invisible certain kinds of work are. Others may not realize what is being carried until it is no longer carried.

Stepping back can be a way of making invisible work visible. It can force recognition of gaps. This can feel uncomfortable and even irresponsible. It can also be necessary for redistribution to occur.

Staying, in contrast, can be a way of preserving fragile structures. In some moments, continuity matters more than ideal conditions. If you are the only person holding memory, access, or process, leaving may cause immediate damage. In those moments, staying may be a deliberate choice to absorb cost temporarily.

The difficulty is that temporary absorption often becomes permanent by default. What was meant as a short-term decision quietly becomes a long-term burden. People tell themselves they will step back later. Later keeps moving.

Another factor is whether the system shows signs of learning. Are concerns acknowledged, even if slowly? Are adjustments made, even if imperfectly? Is there any redistribution of strain? If nothing changes over long periods, staying may simply normalize dysfunction.

There is no formula for this. The same situation can call for different choices at different times. What matters is making the choice deliberately rather than letting inertia decide.

People also need permission to leave without disappearing. Stepping back does not have to mean cutting all ties. It can mean reducing scope, changing roles, or shifting to lower-intensity forms of participation. Return should remain possible.

This is where earlier roles intersect. Boundary setting makes stepping back survivable. Re-engagement makes return possible. Continuity makes transitions less disruptive. Monitoring helps identify when staying is masking drift. Translation helps others understand what is happening. These roles shape whether stepping back or staying has constructive effects.

When people feel trapped between burnout and guilt, both staying and leaving feel wrong. Naming this tension can itself be useful. It shifts the question from moral judgment to structural evaluation.

Staying is not always loyalty. Leaving is not always abandonment. Both can be forms of care, depending on context. The harder question is whether your presence is helping the system become more functional or simply helping it endure without changing.

That question cannot be answered once. It has to be revisited. Capacity changes. Systems change. Roles change. What was once sustainable may no longer be. What was once futile may become meaningful.

Knowing when to step back and when to stay is not a skill people are taught. It is learned through experience, often through mistakes. This chapter does not offer a rule. It offers permission to treat the decision as part of the work rather than as a personal failure.

THE LONG VIEW

CHAPTER 16
The Long View

The Long View

The Long View

Most people do not enter civic life thinking in decades. They think in terms of immediate needs, short-term conflicts, and problems that feel close enough to touch. The long view is rarely available at the beginning. It emerges over time, often through fatigue, disappointment, and persistence.

Systems that last are not held together by constant urgency. They are held together by people who continue after urgency fades. The work described in this book is designed for that reality. Attention comes and goes. Crises burn hot and then recede. What remains is maintenance.

Taking the long view does not mean lowering standards or accepting deterioration. It means recognizing that most change is incremental and uneven. Small shifts accumulate. What feels like stagnation may be slow adjustment. What feels like momentum may be fragile.

People who stay long enough often develop a different relationship to progress. They stop looking for decisive moments. They start noticing whether things are still reversible. Whether channels remain open. Whether memory is preserved. Whether return is possible. These are not inspiring metrics. They are survival metrics.

The long view also changes how people think about success and failure. A setback is not always a defeat. A quiet year is not always a loss. Sometimes what matters most is that something did not collapse. That a fragile structure remained intact long enough for conditions to change.

This perspective can feel unsatisfying in a culture that rewards visibility and speed. It can also feel lonely. People doing long-term maintenance rarely get recognition. Their work becomes visible mainly when it is absent.

Over time, the long view can reduce emotional whiplash. Instead of being pulled by every crisis, people learn to ask whether a moment changes underlying conditions or simply creates noise. They learn to distinguish between events that require immediate response and patterns that require sustained attention.

The Long View

This does not mean disengaging from urgency altogether. Some moments do require intense focus. Others feel urgent because systems are structured to produce urgency. The long view helps separate those.

Another feature of the long view is humility. People who stay long enough see cycles repeat. They see reforms that resemble earlier reforms. They see conflicts that echo older conflicts. This can create cynicism. It can also create perspective. Recurrence does not make problems less serious. It changes how people approach them.

The long view also clarifies limits. No one carries this work forever. Everyone's capacity changes. The point is not to be indispensable. The point is to contribute in ways that allow others to enter, leave, and return. Longevity is collective, not individual.

This is why the roles in this book emphasize function rather than identity. You are not a monitor forever. You are not always a translator or an interruptor or a continuity holder. You do what fits now. Later, something else may fit. The system survives because people move, not because they stay fixed.

The long view also makes room for unevenness. Some years matter more than others. Some contributions are small and still necessary. Some efforts fail and still teach. Over time, people who stay involved learn to carry both disappointment and persistence without turning either into identity.

Democratic systems are not sustained by constant belief. They are sustained by repeated, imperfect effort. They persist because enough people continue doing unglamorous work after belief has been tested.

This book does not offer a strategy for winning. It offers a way of understanding what makes continued participation possible. It does not promise outcomes. It describes conditions.

The long view is not inspiring in the usual sense. It is grounding. It reframes civic life as something closer to care than to conquest. Care is repetitive. It is rarely finished. It is noticed most when it stops.

If there is a single claim behind this book, it is this: democracies persist not because people feel strongly, but because enough people continue doing specific kinds of work after feeling fades. That work is not dramatic. It is not heroic. It is often invisible. Over time, it is what remains.

WHEN THE SYSTEM IS THE TARGET

CHAPTER 17
When The System Is The Target

WHEN THE SYSTEM IS THE TARGET

When The System Is The Target

Most of this book has described civic work under ordinary strain: overload, turnover, limited resources, and conflicting demands. These are familiar pressures in any long-running institution. Under those conditions, the kinds of roles described here function as maintenance. They slow deterioration, preserve memory, translate complexity, and absorb friction so that systems can continue to operate. In those circumstances, the work is difficult but intelligible. People can usually tell what they are trying to protect and why.

There are, however, moments when strain is no longer the right frame for what is happening. There are periods when the system itself becomes the object of pressure. Procedures may still exist, but their purpose begins to shift. Continuity remains, yet what is being continued is no longer what it once was. From the outside, everything can look normal, while from the inside something feels misaligned, even if it is difficult to name precisely. The surface of the institution remains familiar, but the logic underneath it begins to move.

This chapter is about that shift. It does not offer tactics, strategies, or instructions. Its purpose is to describe how institutional capture is experienced from the inside, and how ordinary civic work can take on a different meaning when institutions are no longer merely stressed, but gradually repurposed. The point is not to draw bright lines, but to make visible a change in context that alters the ethical and practical meaning of the work people are being asked to do.

It helps to distinguish between institutions under strain and institutions under capture, because most dysfunction initially looks like strain. Underfunding, staffing shortages, burnout, inconsistent leadership, and political interference that is clumsy or temporary can all create frustration and failure without necessarily changing what an institution is for. In those situations, people work to stabilize, repair, and adapt. The underlying purpose of the institution is still assumed to be intact, even if execution is flawed.

Capture is different. The outward structure remains, but the internal logic begins to change. Rules may still be followed, but selectively, and oversight may still exist even as it becomes thinner and more symbolic. Authority is not removed so much as quietly relocated. Memory is not erased, but it loses standing, precedent becomes optional, and language stays the same while meaning shifts underneath it. The institution looks familiar, but it is no longer oriented toward the same ends.

From the outside, this kind of change can be difficult to see. Meetings still happen. Reports are still written. Procedures are still referenced. The work continues. The difference is not in whether work is happening, but in what that work is now serving. From within, capture is rarely experienced as a single event. It is felt as a pattern of small adjustments that accumulate over time.

Certain questions become harder to ask. Some topics are treated as settled before they are discussed. Definitions of professionalism begin to narrow what can be raised, challenged, or documented. Decisions that once required explanation start arriving without one. These shifts are often subtle. Each one can be defended on its own. Together, they change the institution's center of gravity.

Memory often becomes a liability rather than a resource. People who remember how things used to work may be described as resistant to change. Documentation becomes harder to locate. Turnover is framed as renewal, even when it removes people who understand how safeguards function. The organization may describe itself as moving forward, even as the practical ability to notice, question, or correct drift becomes weaker.

For people doing civic maintenance work, this is often where confusion begins. The roles they occupy still exist. Translation is still needed, continuity still matters, and process still has to run, even as the meaning of that work begins to shift. The same kinds of labor that sustain institutions under strain can be repurposed under capture.

Continuity can begin to normalize what used to be abnormal, while translation softens or obscures what is actually changing. Process can provide cover for decisions that would not have held up under earlier standards, documentation can become selective, and memory can be treated as expendable in the name of efficiency or modernization. The work itself remains familiar, even as the purpose it serves shifts underneath it.

From the inside, this often feels like being asked to do one's job slightly differently in ways that are hard to articulate but easy to sense. The habits, skills, and sense of responsibility that once protected the institution can now be used to stabilize something that no longer deserves stabilization. The work does not disappear. It is redirected.

This is one reason institutional capture is so difficult to confront. It does not require people to abandon their roles. It requires them to perform those roles under altered assumptions. The same professionalism, the same commitment to keeping things running, and the same willingness to absorb strain can now help normalize changes that undermine the institution's original purpose.

A person who carries continuity may be asked to protect arrangements that should be questioned. A person who translates may be asked to make something sound more reasonable than it is. A person who manages process may be asked to treat procedural compliance as sufficient, even when substance has shifted. None of this is described as erosion. It is framed as adaptation, pragmatism, professionalism, or the cost of getting things done.

For people inside institutions, this creates an ethical problem that does not resolve cleanly. Staying can mean becoming part of a system that is being used in ways that conflict with its original purpose. Leaving can mean abandoning what safeguards remain. Speaking up can carry professional and personal risk. Remaining silent can feel like complicity. Continuing to do one's role "well" can stabilize something that should not be stabilized. These pressures do not line up neatly, and they do not resolve themselves.

There is no universal rule that settles this, and people respond in different ways. Some try to preserve fragments of institutional integrity, while others attempt quiet resistance. Some adapt in order to survive and, without intending to, become enablers. Others leave, or stay and become isolated, or burn out over time. What matters here is not prescribing a response, but recognizing that the meaning of civic work changes when institutions are being hollowed out rather than merely stressed.

This is where the idea of civic workers as neutral functionaries breaks down. Under capture, maintenance is no longer neutral. It becomes politically and morally charged, even if it still looks procedural. The work does not announce its new meaning. People have to infer it from patterns, pressures, and the narrowing of what can be questioned.

One of the most difficult aspects of capture is that it rarely produces a single moment that clarifies everything. There is no obvious threshold, no announcement, and no clean break. People inside systems often spend long periods unsure whether what they are seeing is mismanagement, political pressure, temporary leadership, or something more fundamental. They are trained to fix problems, not to diagnose capture. They are trained to give institutions the benefit of the doubt.

By the time patterns become unmistakable, many of the safeguards that would have made a difference are already weakened. That does not mean earlier recognition was easy or obvious. It means ambiguity persists longer than outsiders expect. That ambiguity is not a failure of perception. It is part of how capture works.

The roles described in this book are not immune to this shift. None of them carry automatic moral authority. They are forms of labor, not guarantees of democratic integrity. Under ordinary conditions, they help systems endure. Under capture, they can be distorted, redirected, or used as cover. This does not mean these roles are wrong. It means they are contingent. Their meaning depends on what the institution is being asked to serve.

This is why this chapter comes at the end. The book has focused on making civic labor visible under ordinary conditions, because most people never learn to see it at all. But visibility without boundaries is incomplete. There are moments when the logic of maintenance no longer holds. When continuity is no longer a neutral good. When keeping things running is not the same as keeping them legitimate.

Ending here is not a call to action, but an acknowledgment of limits. It reflects the reality that civic work is not only about endurance, but also about integrity. It is not only about process, but also about purpose, and those two do not always remain aligned.

Even under capture, one thing remains consistent. The work does not disappear. The strain does not lift. What changes is what the work is serving. For readers who occupy civic roles, this is not meant to produce certainty. It is meant to make ambiguity legible. It is meant to help name the moment when something begins to feel off, to recognize when the work you are being asked to do no longer aligns with the institution you thought you were supporting, and to understand why that shift is so difficult to articulate.

This chapter does not resolve that tension, but it does acknowledge it. Democratic systems are shaped, preserved, and sometimes hollowed out through ordinary work, carried by ordinary people, under conditions that rarely announce themselves clearly. Understanding that will not tell you what to do, but it will help you see more clearly what you are standing inside and what that system is being used to serve.

How Everyday Life Positions People In Civic Roles

APPENDIX

How Everyday Life Positions People in Civic Roles

How Everyday Life Positions People in Civic Roles

People rarely experience themselves as "roles." They experience themselves as parents, staffers, retirees, teachers, professionals, caregivers, or neighbors. The language of roles can feel abstract until it is connected to everyday situations and constraints.

This appendix is not meant to assign identities. It is meant to show how ordinary life circumstances often pull people toward certain kinds of civic work. Many people will recognize themselves in more than one pattern. Most people will move between these over time. These are not recommendations. They are patterns that tend to appear in practice.

Parents and caregivers often enter civic life through schools, childcare, healthcare, and community safety. Their involvement is usually time-constrained and emotionally charged. They care deeply, but their availability is uneven. In these settings, parents frequently become monitors. They notice small changes in policies, communication, schedules, or expectations that affect children. They see drift early because they are close to day-to-day impact.

They also often become translators, explaining school decisions or institutional language to other parents in more practical terms. Group chats, informal conversations, and parent networks become translation channels. Many parents also become re-engagers without intending to. They are the ones who reach out to parents who stopped showing up, missed meetings, or pulled back. They lower the social cost of return by normalizing inconsistency. Boundary setting is common in this group as well. Parents often learn to limit involvement to what is sustainable alongside caregiving.

Staffers and mid-level professionals often operate inside systems without full decision authority. They see how procedures actually work and where formal rules diverge from practice. These individuals frequently become translators, explaining internal decisions to external stakeholders or explaining external concerns to internal teams. They live in the space between official language and practical reality.

How Everyday Life Positions People In Civic Roles

They also often become institutional stewards, preserving process credibility from inside. They explain why procedures exist while also seeing where they fail. They carry the tension between loyalty to mission and awareness of institutional limits. Some staffers become interruptors when their role gives them a formal checkpoint. Compliance review, approvals, sign-offs, and quality control functions often turn into interruption points. Boundary setting can be especially difficult for staffers, particularly when job security or advancement is at stake. Those who manage to set limits often become informal models for sustainability.

Retirees and semi-retired individuals often bring time, experience, and lower professional risk. They may also bring long institutional memory. In many settings, retirees become continuity holders. They stay involved long enough to carry memory across leadership changes and volunteer turnover. They remember how things used to work and why.

They also often become monitors, simply because they have the capacity to pay sustained attention. They attend meetings consistently and notice gradual changes. Some retirees become institutional stewards, especially if they previously worked in related fields. They understand formal systems and can explain why certain procedures matter. Re-engagement work is also common. Retirees often reach out to people who have drifted away and make return feel low-pressure.

Teachers and educators operate inside systems that are both highly structured and deeply personal. They see how policy translates into lived experience. Many become translators, connecting policy language to classroom realities for parents, administrators, and communities. They also frequently become monitors, noticing shifts in standards, discipline practices, funding priorities, or administrative expectations.

Some educators become interruptors, especially when they use formal processes to challenge decisions that affect students or staff. These interruptions may take the form of grievances, formal objections, or procedural appeals. Boundary setting is critical in this group. Many educators learn to limit how much emotional and time labor they absorb simply in order to remain in the profession.

Burned-out former activists often carry deep experience and mixed feelings about return. These individuals frequently become boundary setters, consciously limiting scope to avoid repeating burnout. They may also become monitors, staying aware without full immersion. This allows continued connection without total re-entry.

Some become re-engagers, particularly for others who are burned out. They understand the emotional cost of return and are often effective at lowering it for peers. Their history can also make them informal institutional stewards, especially if they understand how movements and organizations fracture over time.

Politically cautious professionals often care but must manage exposure carefully. These individuals frequently become monitors, tracking developments without visible leadership. They may become translators in private or semi-private spaces, helping others understand what is happening without public advocacy. Some become quiet continuity holders, maintaining connections and records without taking on visible roles. Boundary setting is often built in for this group. Limits are shaped by professional constraint rather than personal preference.

Community volunteers and neighbors often enter without clear structure. In these settings, people frequently become continuity holders simply by being the ones who keep showing up. They also become re-engagers, because relationships are local and personal. Return is often social rather than formal. Some become interruptors in small ways, slowing decisions in neighborhood or volunteer contexts by asking questions or requesting clarification.

This mapping is not a test. It is a way of recognizing patterns. If you see yourself in more than one pattern, that is normal. If your roles have changed over time, that is expected. If you do not recognize yourself in any single description, that does not mean you do not fit. It likely means your situation is more specific.

The purpose of this appendix is to make it easier to say, "Given my life and constraints, this is the kind of work I already tend to do," and to see that as legitimate civic contribution.

It is also a way to notice gaps. If everyone in a setting fits the same pattern, certain kinds of work may be missing. That absence is not a moral failure. It is a structural vulnerability.

Civic systems are not sustained by ideal participants. They are sustained by real people working within real limits. The question is not whether you match a role perfectly. The question is whether the kinds of work described in this book are being carried by someone.

When they are, systems last longer. When they are not, strain concentrates until something breaks. Recognizing where you already fit is often the first step in understanding both your value and your limits.

THE END

www.ingramcontent.com/pod-product-compliance
Lightning Source LLC
Chambersburg PA
CBHW070639030426
42337CB00020B/4075